You can read all my books on Kindle for free without printing.

Copyright. All Rights Reserved.

Table of Contents

Introduction

Each year the number of children diagnosed with learning disabilities skyrockets from the previous year. In fact, many of these cases are being diagnosed simply because the "experts" are able to profit of these diagnoses. Although there are many experts that are genuinely concerned about the child's welfare, there are those who are falsely diagnosing many children.

Learning disabilities actually extend beyond an inability to learn certain subject areas or actions; many actually extend to other conditions whether they are mental illness, behavioral problems or other disorders that are attached to learning disabilities. To understand learning disabilities fully, you must do some research of your own. Do not simply take an "experts" word on the fact that you or your child may have a learning disability. Research must be conducted so you know exactly what you are dealing with.

This eBook is designed to provide you with some of that information and research and to help you understand learning disabilities, the various types and how to deal with them.

Chapter 1

Learning Disabilities – A Brief History on Development and Understanding

As a child grows they are learning many new concepts and behaviors. In some instances, confusion will develop and actually hinders the child from learning certain behaviors. Most children are able to work through this confusion, but others are not and they find it difficult to learn certain skills. This tends to occur more frequently in boys, as there are often certain areas that their fathers expect them to pick up quickly. Most fathers do not even realize the learning demand they place on their children and do not know what is occurring under the surface in the child's brain.

When a child goes to school they are bombarded with several different subject areas. They have reading, writing, math, science, social studies and other subjects that they are expected to learn. Many children will have set their own learning goals to meet and become confused by this influx of additional information. Many children may struggle with learning these topics because they are trying to meet the expectations of others, namely their parents and quite often their fathers in particular.

Many children will lean more towards science and become confused with the other information presented to them. Many children will also move towards math because they are able to see the relationship between the two subjects and that most scientific studies are based on mathematical statistics.

Later on down the road, the child will begin looking for a role model. For many children it is one of their parents. For others, it is a TV character. However, when the child is told that TV characters are not real or fictional, they begin to seek out a real life role model based on the characteristics that their TV role model encompasses. This begins to cause even more confusion in the child's mind because he is unable to locate such a person. But the child will still look towards their parents for this role model. Let's say dad has a job that entails a lot of physical activity and he works 50 hours a week. Each night when he comes home he is utterly exhausted. The child will begin to notice each and every detail in the way dad acts when he comes home from work. The child then tries to compare him to his TV character to determine if the TV character is really fictional. Then the child begins searching for what he wants to be in life. All of these various thoughts and comparisons combined with school activities and information becomes a whirlwind of confusion for the child. The child will often forget about his own struggles and will try to please everyone else. On top of all of this there is peer pressure from other children at school. The child is told by them that if he doesn't try to be like everyone else then he is not normal. This is the beginning and the many stages of the development of learning disabilities in a child.

The term learning disability in itself is somewhat of an understatement and doesn't quite encompass all that a learning disability is. After all, we all struggle in life with some sort of learning disability. You may not be very good in math, but you are excellent in English and art. Or, you might be able to learn anything; it just takes you a little longer than others. These types of learning disabilities are completely normal, natural and occur in all people in one form or another. Simply because we are not as quick to catch on as others can cause a person to be labeled with a learning disability, even if you are not really disabled in any way. There are many examples of this in life. For instance, people with learning disabilities were often called "dumb" or "retarded." Later, through scientific reviews, scientists were able to show that the handicapped actually had a lot that they could teach us. Those who were regarded as mentally disabled or retarded were thought to be failures, but we now know that many handicapped children are capable of learning, they just do so at a slower rate and require different teaching techniques.

Science is still working on categorizations for individuals who have learning disabilities. Many are due to mental conditions, while others are physical conditions causing the disability. Mentally handicapped individuals simply have a different way of learning and require different teaching techniques. If appropriate education and teaching techniques are used, the individual will still learn. These individuals can also benefit society in many ways as well. These children are actually different than the child we described above. These people are actually living in a completely different world from you and me, one that can be likened to that of a completely different reality, one that is far different from your own.

However, throughout history we have seen individuals with learning disabilities be treated in a cruel and even inhumane manner. Because of this, even modern children today believe that it is okay to treat these children in a similar manner. Throughout history, individuals who are mentally handicapped have been removed from society, placed in institutions, and even beaten or tortured regularly. Granted, this behavior does not occur today, but the negative point of view towards these people still remains and children can often be even crueler to these individuals causing mental anguish for their victim.

There are ways to overcome learning disabilities. One simple tool that can be utilized immediately is to use "self-talk." Self-talk can help a person discover who they are and what they want to achieve. As the individual works through a problem they can tell themselves the steps that they are working through so that they can focus on the task at hand. Other skills such as observational skills, investigative skills and learning in general at the person's pace can help them to begin working on their learning curve. Learning and collecting evidence is an effective method of learning. It is also beneficial to learn about the different types of learning methods. Visual, hands-on, auditory and a combination of these are effective methods of learning and you will want to discover the types of learning methods that are easiest for you or the child to learn.

Learning Disability Diagnosis Inconsistencies

Children that are diagnosed with a learning disability are often considered to also be disabled due to their inability to learn certain subject areas or skills. Many children are diagnosed when they first exhibit problems learning in a certain area, such as in reading comprehension. Many people have their own unique way of learning and others do their best to conform to the controlled standards of learning that is presented in many schools. Some individuals refuse to allow others such as teacher, political leaders and other people in influential places affect their mind. Other people will investigate and use their creative minds; this is something that is rarely utilized in schools. A person who is not interested in creative art, writing or another creative area rarely uses their creative mind's abilities. Therefore, a child who shows mild symptoms of a learning disability are often diagnosed of a learning disability and may reach the point to where they are essentially tortured by mental health experts afterwards.

The problem with mental health experts is that they range in their abilities. There are those individuals who seem to be "out in space" while others are truly quality therapists. It can be a frustrating experience working with counselors and therapists, but once you find someone you click with and you seem to be getting results with then that will be the person you want to stick with. Not all counselors are alike and many are more concerned with following the code of ethics and the route that other counselors deem as "normal" or the correct way of doing things instead of allowing their own intelligence and intuition guide them through the correct steps. This is what makes the more intelligent individuals who have been diagnosed with learning disabilities different from the rest. Instead of simply believing what they are told and going along with it, they seek out information on the condition and they seek out facts to support their diagnosis. Often these individuals find the reading materials to be more confusing than informative and they notice the faulty facts in this material. So in essence, you must wonder if learning disabilities are a result of a breakdown in communication between the child, the tests they are given to diagnose learning disabilities, the counselors and their parents.

A breakdown in communication is one of the most common reasons for failure in diagnoses. Simply looking at the past of diagnosing learning disabilities in the country and provide you evidence of this. If you notice, we look to history for information, yet we strive to live for the future. Anyone who looks at the past of the school system in this country will see a lot of contradiction. Contradiction also tends to be another major issue in the country. Children with little stress and without a background of negligence or abuse tend to be less intelligent than those children that do have a background of abuse or negligence. Children with mental illness are often more observant those children without a mental illness. This is due to the experience that the child or individual uses knowledge from past experiences to think on a different level because of that experience. Unfortunately, mental health experts and even teachers often judge the neglected or abused child and will claim that they are mentally ill. The fact that the child is acting out from a learned behavior versus mental illness often makes more sense.

Learned behaviors are something that has caused misdiagnoses by mental health experts for quite some time because they are often inconsistent themselves.

For example, when a therapist notices the oppositional traits in a child, they first consider Oppositional Defiant Disorder as the cause for the behavior instead of a learned behavior that a child uses to get what he or she wants. A child with true Oppositional Defiant Disorder typically opposes a set of rules, such as those presented by educational leaders or other leaders in life. Oppositional Defiant patients will often become extremely aggressive when their beliefs are questioned. Sometimes these individuals will act out aggressively without remorse for the person they are acting out against.

On the other hand, a child with oppositional behaviors will allow these behaviors to come and go as they need them. These behaviors are not as frequent as they would be if the child was suffering from Oppositional Defiant Disorder. These behaviors are learned patterns from experiences in their life. These behaviors are very rarely consistent and this is seen because the person is able to turn them off and on as needed and can function in society normally throughout their life. This is best seen in children who throw temper tantrums. From experience they have learned that if they throw a fit in the middle of the grocery store that their mom or dad will buy them the toy or candy bar just to make them be quiet and not cause a scene. This is a perfect example of a learned oppositional behavior. So, as you can see, learning disabilities are easily over dramatized.

Using Compliments to Help Children with Learning Disabilities

Complimenting children is often the best way to help them through the learning process. Complimenting a child with a learning disability is important because these people are often struggling more than other children. They often have low self-esteem because they don't feel smart, normal or even liked in some cases. They are often centered out and labeled as different from other children and many do not understand why this is so. Additionally, these children can often be confused by the meaning of different. To put it simply, they are confused and a simple compliment can help them through their day and through the process of learning something.

Different, in actuality, is a beautiful thing. Different simply means that the person is completely or partially different than others and it is not bad to be different. In fact, if we were all exactly alike there would be no spice in life. Everybody would be the same and the world would be a miserable place to live. Why would you travel to another country if it looked the same as yours? Why would you create art if it all turned out looking the same? You wouldn't. Therefore, different is good. The problem is that most people can accept that there are different genders, races and ethnicities, but when it comes to a person have a learning disability and being different mentally, people seem to not be able to comprehend this and they don't want to believe that this type of different is okay. This inability to comprehend that a different mentality is good has sparked hatred amongst people and even wars. It has also caused many mentally ill or mentally different people to be tortured and looked down upon. This is simply people failing to realize that different is good. Even though this prejudice is not as strong as it has been in previous centuries, it still exists to an extent and mentally ill people are still targets for persecution. The fact of the matter is that we are all equal and this is a fact of life that cannot and should not be denied by anyone.

Because many people are missed diagnosed with a learning disability, it is important to understand the true definition of the term. Learning disabilities simply mean that the person might struggle to learn particular subjects, due to mental interruptions. A person with a learning disability will show continuous signs of this disability. However, if a person only struggles in one area, they do not necessarily have a learning disability, just a slower learning process or a hindrance in that area. When a person struggles in a particular skill, it may be that the material they are learning from is actually what is hindering them. For example, beliefs that stem from religious roots, even if a person does not have religious background can cause confusion for a person. Religion is actually the number one area that causes the most confusion for a person. This is because a person has intuition and insight from birth. This gift of intuition and insight actually deteriorates throughout life and influences will often cause a breakdown in beliefs overtime, which may cause a wealth of confusion for those individuals who are unable to work through these disturbances in their belief system.

As a child grows, they are affected and influenced by many persuasive people and behaviors in their life. For many children, they are very intelligent and can easily observe consistency in behaviors and the reactions towards those behaviors. For example, a child will easily recognize the difference between good and bad behaviors. They will also recognize what comes from those behaviors. Again, a child that sees another child throw a temper tantrum and then that child receives a reward from that bad behavior will register that in their mind and will probably later try that same tactic on their own parents. If rewards consistently come from bad behaviors, then that child will learn what bad behaviors work for them and which ones do not.

If a child is suffering with a learning disability and has been diagnosed with a condition such as ADHD, then the child should receive regular medical checks. With regular physiological treatments, many ADHD patients begin to gain greater focus in life. The Diagnostic and Statistical Manual of Mental Disorders IV was correct when it first published information linking ADHD to the central nervous system. However, the symptoms of diagnosis for the condition have leaned toward mental illness and learning disabilities. Therefore, it is important to remember that health professionals are seeking answers themselves, remembering this as a parent can assist you in finding answers for your child. It is also important to realize that many conditions have overlapping symptoms so you should not focus on only one area when there may be other conditions interacting in the body and mind.

You never want to give up on a child that is struggling to learn. The best thing you can do for them is to keep searching for answers yourself and helping them along. If the child attends therapy, do not necessarily believe everything you are told. Take it upon yourself to keep researching the condition yourself, as children that are not allowed to learn are going to suffer from learning disabilities.

The worst thing you can do as a parent or teacher of a child with a learning disability is not allow them to learn. Learning disabilities are often linked to mental disorders, stress, anxiety and other phobias. When children are diagnosed with learning disabilities they are often forbidden to learn up to their abilities. Many children will actually struggle silently throughout school and hide the fact that they are having difficulty learning. Many students are able to hide learning disabilities often by faking or simply not putting themselves in a situation where their lack of skill will be discovered. On the other hand, there are those children who will make it apparent and will ask for help. Other children show their inabilities by acting out with inappropriate behaviors.

An example of this is a young man who struggled with controlling his behaviors. Many people diagnosed the boy with several dangerous conditions, but teachers often noticed that if they played his little "game" then he would actually work better and do well. Many teachers saw that he was a highly intelligent student, although he failed in many areas of school. After other stopped bullying him, the child was able to bring home good grades and do well in school. This is the incredible power of peer pressure. Peer pressure can actually hinder a child from learning. In some cities, many children resort to joining gangs or simply dropping out of school to avoid the wrath of peer pressure. It is easier for them to give up than it is to be made fun for a learning disability. It is also easier for children to drop out of school to simply escape the peer pressure and pressure from others. Many teachers make no progression at all from these children because they simply do not feel that it is worth their effort if these children do not want to learn. These children are placed into a mold of society as being losers, gang members and deviants. In reality, the child may want to learn they just can't handle the pressure from teachers and other students. Instead of looking for answers and trying to help these children, the teachers let them drop out of school and go to the streets for their education. As you can see, prohibiting a child from learning simply does not work.

Many children are held back in school because they do not perform up to the level they are expected to perform at before moving to the next grade level in school. This also causes frustration and pressure in these children. This causes them to feel as though they are failures and often results in them dropping out of school themselves. Other children are good enough at faking their abilities and working the system that they are able to continue moving forward through school. Instead of looking at their situation as negative they are able to persevere through school.

Learning disabilities are often a struggle to understand themselves. Many people will take the word of experts as gold will not search for the truth. Too many times a parent will sit and allow their child's life to be governed by doctors and therapists instead of searching for answers themselves. Instead of searching for their own answers that could prove useful to their child, they tend to wait for someone to bring the answers to them. Children actually crave to learn. They want to know and they want to learn as others do. They want to be encouraged to learn and they want to be helped. If you actively seek out ways to help your child, you will see improvement in their ability to learn, but you must work with them first. Learning new learning strategies yourself will help your child.

Chapter 2

Learning Strategies

Students that have learning disabilities often have difficulty with comprehension. This is because their decoding process is different than of other students. Recently there have been several studies that show how computer related tools are able to help children with learning disabilities. Amongst these tools are pictorial tutoring tools that are coupled with word learning systems. Some experts believe that these disabilities are due to the child wanting to learn the words *too* much. Other experts believe that there are mental ailments keeping the child from learning.

The problem, however, tends to lie somewhere between the child being an individual and education. When a child does not grasp the meaning of words, it simply means the meaning is not clear to them. This is not always true in all learning disabilities, but it is in many.

For example, when working with a woman who suffers from bipolar manic depression, the woman may be eager to learn. However, she may be suffering from an extremely low self – esteem and have almost no self-confidence. These two things will hinder her from learning because she doesn't believe in herself and her ability to learn. Because of this, the woman may have difficulty learning. All because she doesn't believe in her own abilities! Essentially, this woman has a flawed personality and it is holding her back. So, in essence, instead of the depression holding her back, she had a personality disorder holding her back and is an underlying issue.

Another issue that seems to present itself is that some individuals have a lot of emotional scarring involved. These people allow their emotions to take control of their minds. This means that they have many stressors that are keeping them from learning. This results in their mind being in a state of constant chaos and this prevents them from being able to learn. Unfortunately most mental illnesses have different levels of seriousness as well as different symptoms. Some bipolar patients are more severe than others and can learn effectively. Some bipolar patients simply fail to learn because they are in denial. These types of patients fail to see the importance of learning. They feel that the simply have nothing to offer.

Attention Deficit Hyperactivity Disorder (ADHD) patients are another area of study. Attention Deficit Hyperactivity Disorder has been a condition that is the focus of many studies for quite some time. These patients often show signs such as not being able to pay attention and focus. They also have hyperactivity behaviors that may include blurting out comments or inappropriate words that disturb or interrupt others. The patient also tends to not understand why these behaviors are inappropriate. These patients tend to hurt the feelings of others and appear to show disregard for that. They may also claim that they are bored after playing for a short period of time. They rarely show the ability to focus on one task at a time as well. This typically means that they are unable to focus and stay seated at a computer for a long period of time. This also shows that phonics is not necessarily suitable for all individuals.

Most individuals who are diagnosed with ADHD are actually very smart individuals. Their minds tend to be very active and race about 90 miles an hour, which makes it difficult for them to focus. This means that these individuals do not necessarily need to focus in order to learn. They tend to learn more by observation. Observational learning skills are more likely to benefit those individuals who suffer from ADHD. This does not necessarily mean that these individuals do not have a learning disability however. Studies have also proven that ADHDS patients often progress best when they are a part of an individual study program. Children with dyslexia also tend to learn better in this manner. It is important that a child with a learning disability be allowed to focus and taught individually so that they can learn at their level of understanding. This helps the child to live with the disability as well.

Learning to Live with Disabilities

If you have been diagnosed with a learning disability, then you have the choice of accepting it and moving on or you have the choice of letting it disrupt your life. Simply because you are diagnosed with a learning disability, it does not mean you're disabled. You also have the choice of getting a medical examination and begin weeding out any physical problem as well. Many mental health experts and doctors have made mistakes, so it will not hurt anything to do some research and have some medical testing done to see if this learning disability stems from another physical issue. People are imperfect and there are bound to be mistakes made by doctors and in diagnosing. Therefore, if you have been diagnosed, then you want to verify that this diagnosis is true and not a mistake. Some doctors seek out problems and will create one where there may not be one. This is not an uncommon occurrence. Additionally, there are simply others out there who are just trying to gain by your position. So, if you have been diagnosed with a learning disability then it is time to get on Google and do some research.

What if you really do have a learning disability? Let's say you have ADHD. This is a common disability that people are diagnosed with and it hinders you from learning. Just because you have been diagnosed does not mean that you are not going to be able to no longer learn, it will just take you longer. There are many different levels of learning disabilities as well. Many well-known people have also been diagnosed with these disabilities from dyslexia to ADHD and Bipolar syndrome.

Very few people have only a learning disability as well. Many people actually have another mental condition that simply hinders their learning. For example, schizophrenia has a learning disability associated with it. People with schizophrenia are actually removed from reality mentally and they have difficultly learning because they have to fight mentally to get through mental disturbances such as hearing voices, suffering from hallucinations and delusions. They may often have psychotic mind breaks as well. Still, these people are capable of learning – it just takes them longer than others.

Individuals who are mentally handicapped, formally known as mentally retarded, also have learning disabilities. These people have the ability to learn to a large degree, but they are able to learn. They may be restricted in their learning due to interruptions of the body and mind, but it is not impossible for them to learn.

Other learning disabilities are surrounded by breaks from reality. These people are typically known as having Histrionic Personality Types and Psychosis. Borderline Personality patients also undergo a degree of learning disabilities. This is because of their grandiosity symptoms hindering them from seeing the facts. These individuals tend to be self-destructive and even suicidal. They often fail to see when a person leaves them that they are not being left forever. In other words, they have a severe fear of abandonment. Because this fear is so overwhelming, nothing else matters to them and their ability to learn is hindered at a large degree.

Learning disabilities do not always have an attached mental illness. Learning disabilities are often linked to cognitive, linguistics and language. When a person has difficulty in these areas, it's often for a good reason. Unfortunately, it is rarely seen until the mind is forced to start learning outside its realm of understanding.

Many individuals will fall into a pattern of mimicking. They will begin to copy rules and guidelines that have been set by their role models. They will essentially lose contact with their individuality and personality and begin to do only what their role model does. For example, have you ever noticed how all controlling people in the movies all follow the same personality type? This is because people with a controlling personality learn this behavior from other controlling people. The person may be seen as having a learning disability, but really they are following a behavior. Unfortunately, those so called "normal" individuals fail to recognize this behavior and change it before it grows to something that is out of control.

If you are diagnosed with a learning disability it is essential that you do not give up.

Chapter 3

What are Learning Disabilities?

Learning disabilities are simply minds that are different from others. Many of these minds are specially gifted minds in one area while they may have difficulty learning in other areas. When a person has a learning disability they often have to put more effort into comprehension of facts and words. Sometimes it is possible for individuals to try too hard. But, if there is positive persuasion, then it is likely that the person will succeed. Some individuals have a learning curve that requires them to practice in order to learn, this is completely natural. Still, some people are on a learning curve that is set up for them by teachers and this curve does nothing but confuse the person with a learning disability. These people have to learn at their own pace and on their own curve. What happens is that the learning curve that is set for them will simply confuse them and they may be blocked mentally in certain areas.

If a person has a learning disability, it does not necessarily mean that the person cannot learn. They may simply show slowness in a certain subject area, while they may learn quite quickly in another. In order to correct the issues caused by learning disabilities, you must understand that the person is an individual. Individuality is a person that is distinct both physically and mentally, especially in their personalities. Personalities vary from person to person and they are the brilliance of social and personal traits that a person encompasses. Personalities are established through the years by interactions with people. A personality is what sets each person apart from another. Personality tests have been developed to help therapists, counselors and physicians to determine the social and personal traits of the various personalities that there are. There are very few tests for individuality.

There are schools that will find resources to help them teach children who have learning disabilities. Some schools have even began working on a one on one basis with children who have learning disabilities and have worked with teachers to work specifically with these children. Therefore, there may be many options available to a child with a learning disability, but it may cost more to send children to these schools and it may take more attention from the parent to work with the child as well.

New research and curriculums have been developed for these students as well. Many of these have proven to be helpful and effective in helping with learning disabilities in children. New tactics have proven helpful for children with ADHD, Dyslexia and others. Tactics such as phonics have been useful for children who have various different learning disabilities. Most schools have been working with these children to set up a goals system. This helps them to work on short-term and long-term goals. The goals, however, are often too undefined for some children. It is always important to help children understand so that these goals do not cause more confusion for them. Use very basic language as well, as higher vocabulary words can cause confusion in children as well.

There are instances in which children with a learning disability have a hard time comprehending speech as well. If a teacher speaks with too high of vocabulary for a child, the child may become more confused. There are many children who fall into the snare of a learning disability only to have the problem compounded by a teacher who is adding to the problem.

Mental health experts often over define learning disabilities as well. Many feel that if the person has a mild learning disability that they are potential mental patients. In some cases, they often over diagnose as well. For example, many mental health researchers are trying to dissolve Antisocial Personality Disorder and Psychopathy Disorder. This is because although the labels are accurate, the names themselves become confused. Other mental health experts have difficulty diagnosing Multiple Personality Disorder. Some believe that this disorder is a form of Schizophrenia, which it is not. Others believe that the condition is close to a psychotic break of the mind, which is even further from reality of the condition. These individuals actually tend to be rather intelligent individuals who have mental abilities that are far beyond what other people can do at the same age. Some individuals create personalities as young as one year old to escape mentally from trauma and abuse that they are sustaining.

Learning disabilities are sometimes invented and not based on facts. When a child has a learning ability, you must look into all of the details of the symptoms before making a determination.

Now we will look at a few of the more common learning disabilities.

Attention Deficit Hyperactivity Disorder (ADHD) and Associated Learning Disabilities

When a child or person has a tangled web of confusion in their mind, it's nearly impossible for the person to focus. This focus is an essential element that is required for a person to learn. Many claims have been made that this condition is one of the most common learning disabilities in the world. There are various symptoms including:

- Difficulty focusing on tasks or even playtime
- Difficulty hearing
- Organizing difficulties
- Short attention spans
- Forgetfulness
- Carelessness
- Loses properties
- Has difficulty staying afloat
- Illustrates difficulty concentrating on one task
- May include hyperactivity
- Difficulty staying in one place for longer than an hour
- Over activity
- Excessive speaking out of turn
- Fidgety
- Relentless energy
- Interruptive

You can break down the symptoms to see how a learning disability is associated with this condition. For example, ADHD includes difficulty hearing, hand and eye coordination impairments, and other elements that make it difficult for a person to learn – such as focus and concentration. Because of this we have to use special tactics to assist these individuals in learning.

Many doctors will place a person with ADHD on medication such as Ritalin and Adderall. These medications work to a degree, but they also have side effects. In fact, Canada recently passed a law against prescribing Adderall XR. This was due to several deaths caused by the drug. It has been found that many of these drugs cause more problems than they do good. Because of this, it is wise to learn how you can use natural herbs and remedies to treat this condition. Flavay is a common herbal substance that includes Vitamin E, C and Zinc. The Vitamin E helps the body to promote healthy fat cell membranes and Vitamin C enhances the body's requirement of selenium. Zinc has been shown to promote a healthy mind. Other helpful herbs include Spectrient and Concentrated Omega-3. Fish oils have also been found helpful for children.

According to many studies, ADHD will start at youth and continue to affect the individual through their life. It is also said to be a genetic disorder. However, this is not always the case as many children do not show signs until they are teenagers and even as adults.

Dyslexia and Learning Disabilities

Dyslexia is a learning disorder that many individuals suffer from. In the past people suffering from this condition were simply thought to be dumb, but new studies show that these individuals have a lot that they can teach us. Dyslexia is a brain disturbance that decreases the person's ability to interpret language correctly. Some individuals may see words as being backwards while others will start to write backwards. This makes it difficult for these people to function because nothing makes sense to them. However, these individuals often excel in observation.

This condition is another that is often misunderstood as a person not being able to learn. In actuality, these individuals are perfectly capable of being able to learn, they just have to work through their learning curve differently.

Schizophrenia

A person with schizophrenia has a mind that is in a psychotic state. Schizophrenic minds have their own set of beliefs and when cross that line they will make up their own rules. If you cross over their beliefs, you can easily put yourself in a dangerous situation.

Many individuals with schizophrenia hear voices outside of their heads and tell them that "you are out to get me." These voices put the person in a state that causes them to be convinced their life is in danger. Paranoid schizophrenics have Grandiosity Personality, which can cause a person to want to fight instead of cower. In some cases, schizophrenias have killed others because they were in fear that someone was out to get them.

Now, you may be wondering how you teach a person with this disability. These individuals also have a very real learning disability as well. These people are not stupid by any means and when they are not hallucinating they are very much aware of the world around them and they are able to learn.

When a schizophrenia outbreak does occur, however, it is apparent from the look in their eyes. The look appears to be dead and even evil. During this state, the person has no ability to learn as their mind is clogged with hallucinations, voices and illusions. This condition is one of the most complex mental conditions that has left many experts at a loss.

There are new medications that claim to help with these psychotic breaks. The problem with teaching during these times is that the person believes they are right and you are wrong. Some schizophrenics may even go as far as believing you have a master plan to destroy them and that you are their enemy. Many individuals with this condition will frequent institutions due to their outbreaks and the opportunity for learning there is often very limited.

Another issue with teaching a person such as this is that when they are not in psychotic mode they are very convincing. They have even fooled lying detector machines into believing that they are normal and that there is nothing wrong with them. This poses a serious threat to researchers who are trying to learn more about this condition.

When a person is in symptom mode, you have better luck getting a wall to talk back to you than you have trying to teach anything to the individual. This is the only mental condition with a learning disability that the person cannot learn during without medication. The problem is that many of these individuals will rebel against taking medications. Also, if the wrong medications are prescribed, you are placing yourself in a very dangerous position.

Whether or not these individuals can learn depends on the type of schizophrenia they possess. Paranoid schizophrenics are very complicated individuals and it is difficult to teach them and it is difficult for them to learn. Some researchers believe that a person can be schizophrenic without a learning disorder, but this is questionable.

Understanding Auditory Processing Hyperactivity Disorder

Attention deficit disorder may also be known as Auditory Processing Hyperactive Disorder. This is a complicated condition in which the individual has a hard time understanding and making sense of auditory stimulus. Thus, they have a hard time learning.

Auditory Process Hyperactive Disorder is an epidemic problem that many individuals suffer from. The Auditory Process Hyperactive Disorder affects thousands of adults and children. Symptoms typically include:

- Inability to use common sense
- Habitually verbalize forwardly without concern of hurting other's feelings
- Sense of intense boredom
- Impulsive outbursts
- Act before thinking about consequences
- Disregard consequences of their actions by making excuses for their behavior

This condition is often active because the cranial nerve joins the inner ear, connecting to the brain and transferring impulses, which also controls the balance in the hearing and creates a learning disability.

Once hyperactivity increases, the symptoms of the condition may expand to include behavior that is out of control. The problem is that the person's hearing is off balance and the central nervous system is has hyperactivity explosions, voiding any ability to think positively or clearly.

It is also important that treatment is consistent to avoid complications. Unfortunately, many individuals with this disorder resort to alcohol and or drugs to find relief. Drug and alcohol may increase suicidal tendencies in these individuals. It is important that these people avoid substances to avoid additional problems. Alcohol and drugs affect the brain as well and can decrease the ability to learn as well.

Chapter 4

Disabilities that Hinder Learning and Working through Them

Learning is a slow process that is something that we have worked for years to understand. Many people have a gifted mind and are able to understand a plethora of subject areas, while others are able to specialize in certain subjects while others struggle with several different topics. Some people might be great in English, but fail in math, while others are the complete opposite.

For example, a woman who dropped out of school earlier in life than most and began having children early may not have the best formal education, but she has observed life and learned how to get by on her level of education. In other words, she has learned by observation and experience. This woman could be smart as a whip and even manage her money well.

As you can see, all people learn differently. Education is wonderful, but sometimes education lacks in reality. Teachers are great, but sometimes they are not able to always help. It is often difficult for teachers to help people get up to their level of understanding and sometimes it is difficult for a teacher to drop down to the child's level of understanding. Some teachers are often hard to understand as well. There are several instructors that make no sense at all.

This should you lead to encourage others with a learning disability to not give up. They should consider all possibilities. It is important that you do not set yourself up for failure. If you are struggling to learn or if your child is struggling to learn then it is smart to get a physical and mental evaluation completed. Once you understand the issue at hand you will be better able to move ahead.

If you are suffering from something like ADHD, make sure you grasp the deeper meaning of the condition. It is important to know what is going on in your body and what you reactions are to it. When you are prescribed medication, be ready to argue if you do not feel that you need it. Tell them you want to explore other options.

For individuals who are suffering from learning disabilities it is important that you take care of your body and mind. Research shows that exercise and nutrition are vital in maintaining skills that are needed to learn.

When you try to better yourself you realize how much control you have over your own mind and body. You have control over what you eat, think, feel and do. You are in control of you. If you do not use the list of requirements then most likely you are going to have difficulty learning. Exercise and nutrition also decreases our risk of disease and aging.

Healthy living also enhances your energy level in addition to maintain your metabolism, awareness and helps you to live longer. Everybody wants to avoid disease as well as mental and physical illness. Diabetes, high blood pressure and similar conditions can also cause mind problems which can keep you from learning effectively.

Your body requires a healthy level of carbohydrates, proteins, fats and other nutrients to properly produce insulin and to keep the proper blood flow. Metabolism plays a large part in development as it promotes our energy. This is where you want to consider ADHD as the degree of energy produced in these minds might be linked to over exaggerated metabolism levels. To maintain a level of metabolism that is healthy you must eat healthy foods and get the proper amount of energy on a regular basis. The right type of exercise will also assist you in burning up negative energy.

Cardio exercise is great for burning fat and increasing your metabolism. You often seen ADHD patients benefit more from stretching and mass exercises.

Exercising and eating healthy foods is also beneficial to promote purified oxygen in the body. When your oxygen level is low, it is usually because there are impurities in your system. You need cellular oxygen to cleanse the body and mind to promote learning.

ADHD is the number one learning disability in the country. The diagnosis for this condition has been around for centuries and has been a popular diagnosis as well. In the early 1900's attention deficit disorders were actually known as "Defects of Morality." They were seen as being impulsive behaviors in children that affected their ability to learn. However, these individuals diagnosed were not stupid and they did have a high degree of learning, they just learned more quickly and better on their terms instead of the terms of others.

In other words, a person with ADD did not have to repeat as often or focus for hours on one subject. Because people with ADD have shorter tension spans, it makes sense that they would require less time to learn versus the ordinary minds length of learning time.

It is important to reduce tasks for children suffering from ADHD. Society tries to require that these children measure up to normality, but pushing them can only push them over the edge.

On the other side of this disorder, it appears that the child that is below the learning level fails to use common sense.

This is where something as simple as exercise and nutrition can help a child. Healthy patterns help to develop healthy minds. When a child is lacking in the ability to use common sense then they will need a structural activity to help them focus on controlling their lives.

Conclusion

From the day you are born, you have the ability to see, hear, smell, touch and even relate to those who are around you. A newborn baby can even sense when his or her mother is near them. The baby also has the ability to detect his or her mother's emotions. Therefore, the learning process for a baby begins in the mother's womb.

If a child is raised by a mother who has bipolar depression then the baby will use its mother as an example and act out irrationally as well. If the father is an alcoholic then the child might learn to drink to calm emotions when they are threatened. A child might even resort to alcohol if he or she feels depressed. The child may even believe that happiness is punishable. All of these behaviors go back to how a child sees their parents and uses them as a role model in life.

What children hear and observe are examples of how the child will grow up. The child truly does adapt to his or her environment and they will adjust their behavior to survive. This does not always mean that a child that grew up in a dysfunctional family will have a learning ability, but it does put them at risk for disabilities in life.

People are not singled out in life o suffer more than others. Once a child reaches the age to attend preschool or Head Start the child will meet new people who will give them new rules for life. The rules may influence the child's life and teach them that it is good to be happy and that irrational behavior is bad. Every adult influence in a child's life will influence it – this influence can be either positive or negative. We hope that it is positive.

However, if the rules that the child learns at school conflicts with what they learn at home then there is cause for confusion. If mom acts irrational and has manic depressive attacks and dad drinks excessively when he is stressed, then the child sees the conflict in their life and they don't know what to believe. They don't know whether or not it is good to be happy and they don't know what is going on in life. The child may see that dad goes to the bottle to attain temporary stress relief and the child may then believe that happiness is only an illusion.

So what happens when the child goes back to school? The child sees the rules that the school teaches and compares them with what his or her parents show the child when they are at home. The child may see the school as a "make believe land" and home as a harsh reality.

But the child is then forced to compare the two sets of conflicting rules in his or her life. They see the happy school and the not so happy home. Where are the child's beliefs? Where do his beliefs fall into the picture?

The child's beliefs are rarely seen because everyone teaches the child something different. They are taught to believe in accordance with everyone else. The perfect example of the completely confused child is the one that grows up in a poverty stricken home and is as follows.

The child grows up in a home in which the mother is a paranoid schizophrenic and is "defeated" by the man she calls her husband. The mother teaches her child that boys are better than girls and the child is forced to believe this. The mother also tells the child that she is to be seen and never heard. The child is sometimes even seen as a waste of time to her parents.

The father teaches the child that talking, crying and even being overly happy are bad emotions and that she will get in trouble for any and all of them. The child fears the father and fears showing emotion to the child. If she angers him logically or illogically, she reaps the punishment of it.

The young child is then taught that education is worthless. She is taught that the only value education has is that it is a method used to control the lives of others. To this degree, the man was right as the National Education Association is constructed to rule rather than focus on helping a child learn.

Later, as the child grows, the child sees other children who hurt, mimic, criticize and hurt others. The child watches as teachers stand by and punish the child that was acting in defense against the bullies. The child observes the leaders and how they behave when complex problems are presented.

Now, the woman could learn to act out as the people around her acted. But, she had her own beliefs and decided to stand by them. As you can see, the now grown child has struggled through life and through the complexities in her life that hindered her learning ability. However, the woman learned that by observing, comparing, contrasting, analyzing, and investigating she has learned to find facts to prove her beliefs in life.

This is the type of life that many children lead who suffer from learning disabilities. Now, obviously every child's life is not going to be poverty stricken, but they are going to see the clash in family values and the clash in school values. They are either going to be overcome by confusion or they are going to fight their way through it. Those children who succumb to confusion are more likely to develop some other sort of mental illness or defect. They may suffer from learning disabilities as a result. Other children may only suffer from one or another learning disability as well. Some children will resolve to fight against these disabilities while others will succumb.

What happens to you or your child is completely up to you. You can persevere, find more information, do the necessary research and fight through the disability. Or, you can succumb to the disability and do nothing about it. What you do is completely up to you, but it is important that you realize that it is possible to fight through these disabilities and to learn to whatever degree you desire.